Until I've Forgotten, Until I'm Stunned

Until I've Forgotten, Until I'm Stunned

Poems by

Michael Carrino

© 2019 Michael Carrino. All rights reserved.
This material may not be reproduced in any form, published,
reprinted, recorded, performed, broadcast,
rewritten or redistributed without
the explicit permission of Michael Carrino.
All such actions are strictly prohibited by law.

Cover design: Say Culligan

ISBN: 978-1-950462-21-6

Kelsay Books Inc.

kelsaybooks.com

502 S 1040 E, A119
American Fork, Utah 84003

For Thel

Acknowledgments

The author wishes to acknowledge the editors of the following publications in which these poems appeared:

Catamaran: "The Bird Artist Finds Morning in Newfoundland," "In Stefania's Attic"

Courtship of Winds: "Methods of Painting Waterfalls," "Waiting for Summer in the Northeast Kingdom of Vermont"

Iowa Source: "The Tourist Guide Poet in Shiga Prefecture," "Coffee and a Doughnut at Rulf's Apple Orchard on a Mild September Morning in Peru, New York"

Literary Juice: "After Finding a Pitted, Salt-licked White Cadillac for Sale in a Grand Isle, Vermont Barn"

Main Street Rag: "Before the Rain"

Prole: "Magic," "Allison"

Rockvale Review: "The Village of Living Water"

Straight Forward: "Japanese White-eye in Plum Tree"

The RavensPerch: "In the Kitchen Late on a Wednesday Night in April"

The Tower Journal: "Karasu – the Jungle Crows of Tokyo," "Asian Flowering Plum in Full Bloom Under Moonlight," "Where You Find Hints of Possible," "At Hardwick House," "Out of the Past"

Trajectory: "At the Cherry Blossom House"

Contents

The Bird Artist Finds Morning in Newfoundland	11
Waiting for Summer in the Northeast Kingdom of Vermont	13
In the Kitchen Late on a Wednesday Night in April	15
After Finding a Pitted, Salt-licked White Cadillac for Sale in a Grand Isle, Vermont Barn	18
Asian Flowering Plum in Full Bloom Under Moonlight	19
At the Cherry Blossom House	20
Methods of Painting Waterfalls	21
The Tourist Guide Poet In Shiga Prefecture	23
The Village of Living Water	25
The Sika Deer of Nara Park	26
Karasu—the Jungle Crows of Tokyo	28
Japanese White-eye in Plum Tree	29
Where You Find Hints of Possible	30
At Hardwick House	31
Magic	32
A Man Walks Into a Bar	33
Before the Rain	36
September	37
Allison	38
Out of the Past	39
In Stefania's Attic	40
Coffee and a Doughnut at Rulf's Apple Orchard on a Mild September Morning in Peru, New York	42

The Bird Artist Finds Morning in Newfoundland

...I imagine, lost in thought, when she saw me and was overcome.
            —Howard Norman

A purple slash of light licks ash-stained sky
as I try to rise, check

each black hand on the bedside clock
for the hour, yet it's plain

dawn is breaking coarse. I write one line
of a letter to Chiyo interrupted

yesterday. Now, beginning another
I brew coffee, leave the local

paper on my doorstop, no interest
in expert opinion, odd

bits of rumor, misnomer. Later, in blurry
mid-day light I will navigate

the sea wall path, the lighthouse and cliff
still coated with the last

stubborn mist, find myself imagining honest
labor at the dry dock, and as

too often lately, fancy myself a bird artist.
Drawings of ibis and osprey, already

sold this year to patrons in Halifax. Puffin
and two harlequin close

to complete. Workers will be drying
cod, as children fish

off the salt-bleached pier. The Lady
Marguerite Barnacle

will leave the wharf. I'll add for possible
future reverie a more

favorable wind. I'll have black-backed gulls
marauding off its bow.

One of Chiyo's letters in each beak.

Waiting for Summer in the Northeast Kingdom of Vermont

I, Alvy, hope someday, someone is impressed that I lived in the Northeast Kingdom for some time.
—journal entry

Summer will be easy warm and azure blue
when it can arrive. It will
drift through September, try to linger

into October, and only fall, along with each
compelling, dying leaf.
Another long, stone-gray winter, and again

one more lost spring, its possibility
vague in wet, slant
memories, on nights like tonight, a night

cold and leery, a feral cat curled
in a dim lit corner
too long before dawn. I, Alvy, roam

the house imagining Jake, once
a friend, lingering
at The Gap Pub and Grill in Westmore

near Lake Willoughby, where he spills
clichéd angst, half-hearted
regret, to no one in harsh closing time

light and then I find myself staring
through my bedroom
window, where I find nothing

but night, must imagine boreal forest,
moonlight, remember
summer will be easy warm; azure blue

when it can arrive. Each languid day
counted to allow

summer to feel endless, counted
slowly as if

to slowly lull me
away from one more memory.

In the Kitchen Late on a Wednesday Night in April

I, Alvy, do not like to travel. Oh, and I am haunted by loud memories.
—journal entry

I'm tired. The moon is full; its light
dapples Lake Champlain.
It's quiet until, but as usual,
Pelagea and Tino, upstairs neighbors
in this apartment hive,
begin a loud argument. Tonight
it's where to travel. Pelagea favors
Japan, Tino, China.
They argue often, and often, for more
serious reasons. Worrying, I'm now
imagining them both
whispering to each other, then anyone
who will whisper back, until
more lovers and friends begin
to whisper, until whispering
feels natural, muffling
all but a hint of every
grouse, secret, or threat
shouted through ceilings, into
cell phones on any street, to
anyone, perhaps a barista
in a café. At last
I will overhear less
accusations, reckless gossip
concerning any fraying marriage,
impotent doubt, or lament
festering in bleary, ragged memories
regarding what one
stranger or acquaintance
might do, might fail to do.

As for Tino and Pelagea, I cannot
hear anything, will not
intrude on anything
I hear. For now
their argument is spent.
Yet, I'm leery their stinging
words are only practice, a prelude.
Now, I find myself
holding a glass half full of water,
staring at patient moonlight.
The stove hood light now a pale
blue shadow on the stained
porcelain sink, where I, Alvy, find
Kate Walbert's novel
In The Gardens of Kyoto, put aside
last night, while
I was distracted by Tino
slamming a door.
One thread of a sentence
floats into my mind, "...think of a thousand
things, lovely and durable
and taste them slowly..."
a wisp of poetry I'm not yet fully
remembering. I imagine
whispering *so it goes, hard cheese,
all in time, yes
all in good time...no, stop,* not
expecting any answer.
Anyone on a street, or alone
at home can feel invisible.
I'm tired, but will

lift Walbert's book, read it
from where I left off,
read words in a whisper, until
I can't help but
drift into this tentative quiet.

After Finding a Pitted, Salt-licked White Cadillac for Sale in a Grand Isle, Vermont Barn

I, Alvy, exploring...
    —journal entry

In this candent heat I jab the pedal
as tires squeal, backend squirrelly, now back in line

through a vicious, hypnotic glare
on U.S. 15. Las Vegas burns my neck, the west coast

too far off for more than imagining
Redondo Beach, Santa Monica, Malibu, Santa Barbara,

as my hung-over hitchhiker, his shy
actress companion, both oblivious, stare into blisters

of desert, while I envision their doubtful
future, the glow of Las Vegas now mere neon mirage

in miserable daylight. Direction,
desire, never in doubt, perhaps closer tomorrow.

Asian Flowering Plum in Full Bloom Under Moonlight

Ambrosial scent on a slight
wind, the lush

garden wet
with dew. Imperfect

beauty of simplicity
as in wabi-sabi

zen art that entices
the most vivid

memories. If I possessed
black ink brushstroke

skill I'd bow to
the task, not resist

the mysterious

abundant fragrance.

At the Cherry Blossom House

Yakisoba—
stir-fried. Hot pepper flakes,

rice vinegar, rice
wine. Myouga.

Miso. Beni shouga, pungent
chives, delighted senses.

Night lingers
in frail moonlight—

sated in jasmine scent.
I caress your pale cheek, breathe

white musk perfume.
Wait—

then wait…
touch your gold anklet

and wait...

Methods of Painting Waterfalls

the brush stops but the spirit continues...
—Wang Gai in *The Mustard Seed Garden Manual*

The ancients said *Take five days to place
water in the picture*

Wang Gai instructed artists to paint until
close to hearing

sounds of water   to remember ping yuan
perspective   how

artists must consider   it vital
Wang Wei wrote

*when one paints a waterfall it should be
painted with some interruptions*

but no breaks   while all ideas
must remain

uninterrupted as one divine dragon
partly hidden

among clouds head and tail one
natural connection

               I often read lazing
on the rock wall

                 above the lake beach
have never seen

                    a dragon   divine
or flawed as all of us

                    much time long gone
since I've seen or heard

                    one waterfall   yet in reverie
can hear its echo and roil

                    I cannot paint this lake
by moonlight   dark

                    cloud about to part
and certainly not any waterfall

                    yet in one calm silence
I believe I might feel

                    waterfall mist touch
no   caress

my dry palms

The Tourist Guide Poet In Shiga Prefecture

> *...Another must...Ishiyama-dera Temple...along the west bank of the Seta River...This temple is not renowned for various important cultural properties and national treasures, but for being the place where Murasaki Shikibu came up with the idea for* The Tale of Genji.
> —Aya Satoh in *The Mainichi*

I find Murasaki Shikibu after another day of service
to the empress at court, in her room watching
moonlight reflect off Lake Biwa, as she casts a tranquil
gaze out her window, as she lifts her brush
to write, and according to lore, sets to work on
this world's first novel. It has been written
Murasaki Shikibu was foremost a poet of unique
talent, not least her facile
taste for irony. Yet emphatically

    it is also written that *The Golden Ass* by Apuleius, one
thousand years older, is the first novel. Mystery
and debate arise due to bias, historical neglect, dearth
of precise knowledge. Perhaps
some puzzling combination.

    Search with more care if you desire better truth. Much
can be lost over time, or in translation. I doubt
Murasaki Shikibu would find your curious interest
in this matter rude or spiteful, since
every first is the first we find. Yet now

                  I'm sorry, I've somewhat lost
my way. Murasaki Shikibu can so easily lead
me astray, allow me to forget
always to respect all aspects of my calling—
one reliable, near invisible, guide,
content with my modest craft.

                         So please, when
in Shiga Prefecture, visit Otue the capital
city, Ishiyama-dera Temple, be sure
to read all pamphlets, and of course any useful
words by Aya Satoh. Taste all delicacies
found in Lake Biwa. Ebi, cooked prawns

   mixed with soybeans, excellent Biwa
trout or thin sliced
assorted sashimi. I believe you will surely

   enjoy all such sensual delights, but perhaps
not so well as Murasaki Shikibu's
luscious poetry, her delicious novel.

The Village of Living Water

the Harie district in Takashima
 —Shiga Prefecture, Japan

Hira mountain water joins Lake Biwa, finds a path
to Harie village.

Many homes have Kabata rooms, where carp in deep
basins eat scraps

of rice, tofu, from plates and bowls. There are more
basins where villagers

rinse vegetables, cook food, and savor clean water.
Carp go where they please—

canals, streams, and back to homes, all part of "shozu,"
the living water culture

meant to nourish both villagers and rice fields. All
community and harmony

a desire to conserve, keep precious water pure. Clear
water has a unique flavor

in each household, but is always savory, always fresh.
Curious visitors receive

one hand-made bamboo cup to taste water drawn
from Harie springs. One reminder

it is sweet to drink from your source.

You can keep that cup forever.

The Sika Deer of Nara Park

Nara City, Japan

In the year 768, Takemikazuchi-no-mikoto was enshrined with three other Gods in Kasuga Taisha temple, which still stands today, in Nara Park. Legend has it Gods of the grand shrine have been sending messengers to watch over the city in the form of Sika deer ever since.
—The Incidental Naturalist

When you arrive, Sika deer will always be there
early, so prepare
for them to brush slowly past you, bow their heads
to be fed biscuits.

Sika deer expect special treatment, so long divine
until Hiroshima,
Nagasaki, the end of war. They are at present, only
by decree, a national treasure.

Sika deer might nip, nudge, even bite, or push
you down if you fail
to show a proper respect. If you dare tease
our Sika deer, beware.

Many tourists sustain injury each year despite
numerous warnings
in various languages. But, remember
Sika deer will provide

you bliss, calm you, enhance all healing peace
in Nara Park, where
I was once a tour guide, now long
retired.   One piece

of vital information. For some years
now many Sika deer
in outer zones some distance away
from the grand shrine

have been culled. They are captured, and even
offered to residents as pets, but
most are killed.

This sorrow is not always
known. Those best informed
have made wide inquiries, countless

petitions. Yet, as Sika deer
grow bold, more
at ease, tourist or bureaucrat

will have their way.
Please do not hesitate to visit
Nara, our ancient

temple, our watchful Sika deer
here in the park.

They roam as if
still divine.

Karasu—the Jungle Crows of Tokyo

One Karasu, its covet slick, lifts off a power line, drifts
onto a sidewalk near Ueno Park after a downpour.
It will not be denied a mound of white
plastic bags bloated with last night's trash.
Tourists quickly find what pests these huge crows
have become. In Tokyo
Karasu perch on Cherry Blossom and Pink Sakura,
build nests sculpted of metal hangers
plundered off wash lines.
In rural areas scarecrows are dead carrion crows
hung upside down. In Tokyo a mimic—
plastic crows upside down. Karasu mourn. Their calls a dirge
as they shy away.
There are 35,000 crows in Tokyo.
A surreal presence, even
when official notices and hotel
guidebooks are read with care.

Karasu will have their way amidst refuse and flower.
They are inevitable, even
in the most private air.

Japanese White-eye in Plum Tree

Olive green back. Yellowthroat close to obscure
in a tangle of wet

branches. Brown wings taut, quiet. All impulses mute
in this brief delay more

denial than a pause before more relentless,
inevitable rain.

Where You Find Hints of Possible

White moonlight
        drips across a dim-lit back street

as voices echo
        from an invisible open window.

Jasmine scents trigger
        a continuously puzzling memory—

spices that calm
        in late night tea, shallow breaths

in the churning,
        all too early, Santa Anna wind.

At Hardwick House

Bury St. Edmunds, Suffolk

Past brick pillars, wrought iron gates, at last, the house
an apparition, shrouded

in mist. Once inside hearth fire bathes the great hall
gold, one cut glass

decanter thick with Merlot waits on a serving cart.
High windows still

reveal pleasure grounds—gazebo, peach house, vinery,
a faded path, leading

in time to a rustic cottage, candlelit. Mint tea steeps
in the cold kitchen, its scent

drifting over worn steps leading to one room—
ivory sheets entangle

on the bed, one locked closet, bare
walls, scratched

wood floor, opaque skylight. One
or two-day escape.

Perhaps an indefinite stay.

Magic

Illusions, necessary as breath, collapse
into lie, spite, dazzling

fear and uncertainty. The once deft
coin and card tricks now

derided. Those old delights were rarely
perfect, but always

could suggest what seemed lost
were only hidden.

Each card, coin or truth still
in plain sight,

despite what furious tyrants
loudly insist

must forever vanish.

A Man Walks Into a Bar

I, Alvy, am ambivalent about being a poet, but not always.
—journal entry

What do you get when you combine Robert Frost and James Bond?
The Road Not Taken But Stirred.
—Allen Wolf

I'm incognito, but no one knows
I'm here in Cape May, New Jersey, sitting
on the beach, listening
to roiling waves usher in another
morning, while I consider
giving up poetry to become a comedian.

      "The doctor says, I have bad news
and good news, the bad..."
      "Yes, and such small portions."
      "His instinct when he drops
something is to run away"
      "Who are you
going to believe, me
or your own eyes?"

Words chosen carefully, written and revised,
revised again, and again
over time, until

it's time for a poet or comedian
to recite those words
to an audience. In the end
only one audience is likely laughing.

      "Oh, I love how you
can wear anything."

I, Alvy, am a poet who will
often stand stiffly, ruffling
pages, squinting in low
light, ask meekly
if the bookshop, or library
host has time for me
to read one more
short poem.   Comedians prowl
their stage, are jazz
musicians practiced in tone, pace,
the roiling vibe of any room.

I will go on and on
year after year imagining I've never
had enough time
to write, enough money
for a two week retreat.

          "When does a kid get
to sit in the yard with a stick?"

I, Alvy, must be expert
at handling delayed
gratification or no
gratification.
Comedians crash into taboo.

          "Too soon?"
          "A talent agent is
sitting in his office..."

They sense when serious is a balm,
not wound.

                "I have cancer
how are you?"

Oh, and comedians don't need
to show up daily
at a University, to explain
why a bit, set, any shtick,
story, premise, one
damn joke, is funny.

But, years after a joke is told,
comedians somewhere offstage
know there is a word
they ache to change.   Maybe I'll
remain a poet. I'll decide
after some Cape May Belgian
waffles. Belgian is a funny word.

         "Time flies like an arrow,
fruit flies like a banana."
         "I see the glass as too big."

Before the Rain

Red scent on taut wind. Rain
threatening in thick air. Kerosene and dye, rough

perfume from the paper mill
down Christine Street. Strips of porch light glaze

the stockade fence, granite
backyard path, silent fire pit embers, hammock, two

wine glasses, all those last
dregs of Merlot. Chimes are tangled, and one

French door is ajar.
Red scent persistent. A traffic light fandango

on the electric cable
above Christine Street, pulsing red, yet

no one is around to yield.

September

One imaginary gull hovers above invisible, hushed
waves that lick our lee shore. Morning

heat can't slice a thick mist, burn narrow cobblestone
lanes. Opaque shades are drawn

in this town's one small café. A twisting, slick road
will only breach, dissolve

along each jagged, inarticulate cliff.

Allison

Reading the newspaper in the kitchen
I find she has died, overcome
at fifty-seven by complications,
the bleary light
of the unknown. I recall

her vivid twirling
in a classroom, recall
her as eager and elusive. At times
she found the daily ramble
confusing and amazing, always

turning to embrace
the chime of risk and dare, her voice
often one beat early,
one beat late.
But now, I'm failing

to recall more, failing
to desire one
more memory, as I fold

the paper, tap it
three times on my knee.

Autumn is blazing
outside the window, leaf and dust
a swirl of red, gold.

Winter will arrive
all too soon, its threat

as always, to last forever.

Out of the Past

Remains of autumn light
sift through a bedroom window, bathe

one warm white pillow
with shadows: tree limb, power line,

crow and sparrow
in rushed flight. The narrow bed

is ready to embrace
anyone inclined, entice someone

into one ambivalent
dream, long buried, lost in blistered

reverie now revived

in vivid, biting detail.

In Stefania's Attic

dusk of an August Wednesday, Brooklyn, New York, in the year 1961

The scent of jasmine incense
encircles what remains of daylight. The last
faint streaks drift through one rusted air vent. A dented
biscuit tin heaving with treasure is open on the scarred
oak table—flint, belt buckle, white button, thimble,
marble, wish bone, and more. It's Bedford Avenue. We are
fourteen. Both of us barefoot, waiting

for our bodies to ambush us
this afternoon. You offer one discrete desire. I choose
after my usual hesitation, the white button, grasp it, drop it, pick
it up, push it deep into my dungaree pocket.
You touch my foot.   With so much time between us now
I cannot recall your face, but can retrieve your attic, that tin box
brimming with treasure.

The things we want
come by nature, but if necessary by some ambivalent design.
We were not brave, though I ached
for one of us to be brave. We allowed our lives
to remain the same.   Yet, here is the white button
in a bosun's whistle box, under a scrum of paper clips, one
rubber band, two pencils,

as I reach for my pen.
It is August, as it was August then. It's dusk
on the lake beach, and chilly. Someone has lit coals in a fire pit.
Yesterday I discovered a small blue bottle of Jasmine essential oil
at a gift shop, slipped it

into the pocket of my blue jeans
where it hid all day until I found myself slowly twisting
its tight cap, releasing
one, four, ten thousand memories captive
within its combustible scent.

Coffee and a Doughnut at Rulf's Apple Orchard on a Mild September Morning in Peru, New York

I rarely travel. I don't enjoy
the journey. I'll live like Proust
so often in bed
if friends keep annoying me about
only traveling in my head. I get
what Thoreau wrote: "I have
travelled widely
in Concorde." I've never been
to Concorde, but will
drive to Montreal. Yet, I prefer
riding the train. I enjoy

waiting at the border, that quiet
intrusion as I read, or write
a letter, or study
dark clouds about to burst.
I'll drive to Burlington, Vermont, even
take the ferry across
Lake Champlain if the wind
is not a south wind, the waves too rough.
I'll drive to Saratoga, but not
during the thoroughbred season.
I will not fly anywhere until

I can fly to Japan, and arrange
not ever coming back. I can imagine
boarding a fast train, Tokyo to Kyoto,
blazing light to tranquil
gardens until I die. No roads diverge
in any woods. I don't walk

into forests, or hike
any path, or hill, or mountain.

I'd like to drift along an ocean beach
again someday, if I find
the time to find my way

to Gloucester, Massachusetts, or York, Maine.
I'd love to step into the Pacific
once, in southern California, but
again, that flying, and again not
ever, never, to return home.
But, it's not Japan. It would be
fine, but not Japan.

I'll keep reading, watch too many old
movies, walk the lake beach, this small
city's streets, write letters
to the few friends who still
write letters, even short letters.
Many people must imagine
travel bestows enlightenment. I wonder if

they believe they should travel
more? I don't ask, but most
folks seem to love traveling. They want
to keep moving. I guess
they are excited to scold me, but I'm not
planning on changing, unless
something powerful, or frightening

pulls me to Japan at last.
I've read doughnuts have no redeeming
value and are empty
calories, full of nothing.
I take my coffee black. All that caffeine,
all that sugar, right now
in this doughnut and coffee

has me a bit wired
this morning, but
liking it. I don't often have a coffee
with a warm, fresh
Rulf's doughnut.
I try to wait
a long time between

all petite desires
until I've forgotten, until

I'm stunned
how good nothing can taste.

About the Author

Michael Carrino holds an M.F.A. in Writing from Vermont College of Fine Arts. He is a retired English lecturer at the State University College at Plattsburgh, New York, where he was a co-founder and poetry editor of the *Saranac Review*. He has had six books of poetry published: *Some Rescues, Under This Combustible Sky, Café Sonata, Autumn's Return to the Maple Pavilion, By Available Light,* and *Always Close, Forever Careless,* as well as individual poems in numerous journals and reviews.